First World War
and Army of Occupation
War Diary
France, Belgium and Germany

27 DIVISION
Headquarters, Branches and Services
Commander Royal Engineers
21 March 1915 - 31 December 1915

WO95/2256/3

The Naval & Military Press Ltd
www.nmarchive.com
Published in association with The National Archives

Published by

The Naval & Military Press Ltd

Unit 10 Ridgewood Industrial Park,

Uckfield, East Sussex,

TN22 5QE England

Tel: +44 (0) 1825 749494

www.naval-military-press.com

www.nmarchive.com

This diary has been reprinted in facsimile from the original. Any imperfections are inevitably reproduced and the quality may fall short of modern type and cartographic standards.

© **Crown Copyright**
Images reproduced by permission of The National Archives, London, England, 2015.

Contents

Document type	Place/Title	Date From	Date To
Heading	WO95/2256/3		
Heading	27th Division Divl Engineers C.R.E. Mar-Dec 1915		
Heading	27th Division Hd Qrs RE. 27th Division Vol I.21.3-31.5.15		
Heading	War Diary of Headquarters 27th Divisional Engineers From March 21st 1915 To 31st May 1915		
War Diary	Headquarters 27th Divisional R.E. Reninghelst	21/03/1915	21/03/1915
War Diary	Hd. Qrs. As Above	22/03/1915	24/03/1915
War Diary	Hd. Qrs. 27th Divisional R.E. Reninghelst	25/03/1915	25/03/1915
War Diary	Hd. Qrs. As Above	26/03/1915	28/03/1915
War Diary	Hd. Qrs. 27th Divl R.E. Reninghelst	29/03/1915	29/03/1915
War Diary	Hd. Qrs. As Above	30/03/1915	01/04/1915
War Diary	Hd. Qrs. 27th Divl R.E. Reninghelst	02/04/1915	02/04/1915
War Diary	Hd Qrs. As Above	03/04/1915	30/04/1915
Miscellaneous	Horseguards 7.3.25	07/03/1915	07/03/1915
War Diary		01/05/1915	31/05/1915
Miscellaneous	C.R.E., 27th Division.	28/05/1915	28/05/1915
Heading	2nd Division Hd Q.R.E 27th Division Vol II 1-30.6.15		
Heading	War Diary of Headquarters 27th Divisional Engineers From 1st June 1915 To 30th June 1915		
War Diary		01/06/1915	30/06/1915
Heading	27th Division Hd Qrs RE. 27th Division Vol III		
Heading	War Diary of Headquarters 27th Divisional R.E. From 1st July 1915 to 31st July 1915 Lt. Col C.R.E. 27th Division		
War Diary		01/07/1915	31/07/1915
Heading	27th Division H.Qrs RE. 27th Division Vol IV August 15		
Heading	War Diary Of Headquarters 27th Divisional Engineers From August 1st 1915 To Aug 31st 1915 Capt Adjutant For CRE 27th Div		
War Diary		01/08/1915	31/08/1915
Heading	Hd Qrs RE 27th Division Vol V Sept 15		
Heading	War Diary of Headquarters 27th Divisional Engineers From Sept 1st 1915 to Sept 30th 1915 Lt Col R.E. CRE 27th Division		
War Diary		01/09/1915	30/09/1915
Heading	P.a Ypres 1915 To CRE 27th Division Letter		
Miscellaneous	My dear Edmunds 11.3.23.	11/03/1923	11/03/1923
Miscellaneous			
Heading	Hd Qrs RE. 27th Division Vol VI Oct 15		
Heading	War Diary of Headquarters 27th Divisional Engineers From 1st Oct 1915 To 31st Oct 1915		
War Diary		01/10/1915	31/10/1915
Heading	H.Q. RE. 27th Divn Nov Vol VII		
War Diary	War Diary of Headquarters 27th Division Engineers From Nov 1st 1915 to Nov 30th 1915 Lieut Col		
War Diary		01/11/1915	30/11/1915
Heading	War Diary of Headquarters 27th Divisional Engineers From Dec 1st 1915 to Dec 31st 1915		

War Diary　　　　　　　　　　　　　　　　　　　　　　　　　　01/12/1915　31/12/1915

WO95/22561/3

27TH DIVISION
DIVL ENGINEERS

C. R. E.
MAR - DEC 1915

121/5775.

27th Division

Hd Qrs RE. 27th Division

Vol I. 21.3 — 31.5.15.

Confidential

War Diary
of
Headquarters 27th Divisional Engineers

From March 21st 1915   To. 31st May 1915

Army Form C. 2118.

WAR DIARY
or
INTELLIGENCE SUMMARY.
(Erase heading not required.)

Instructions regarding War Diaries and Intelligence Summaries are contained in F. S. Regs., Part II and the Staff Manual respectively. Title pages will be prepared in manuscript.

Hour, Date, Place	Summary of Events and Information	Remarks and references to Appendices
March 21st 1915. Headquarters 27th Divisional R.E. RENINGHELST.	Lt. Col. H.M. Marshall left to take over Roads in 2nd Corps area. Proceeded to BAILLEUL.	
March 22nd 1915. Hd Qrs as above	Bt. Lieut. Col. G. Walker arrived and took over duties of C.R.E. 27th Division.	
March 23rd 1915. Hd Qrs as above	Capt. E.G. King R.E. attached for temporary duty with 2nd Wessex Field Col. R.E. left to take over duty of Staff Officer to C.E. 2nd Army. 1st Wessex Field Co. leaves DICKEBUSCH & billets at ZEVECOTEN.	
March 24th 1915. Hd Qrs as above	Lieut. R.S. Godsall R.E. attached for temporary duty with 1st Wessex (Field Co.) left to report this a.m.d (1st & field 6th R.E.) Brigadier Gen. Petrie (C.E. 5th Corps) had an interview with C.R.E. with regard to work on G.H.Q. line (near DICKEBUSCH. Lieut. M.C.A. Mille 2nd Wessex R.E. awarded Military Cross.	

Army Form C. 2118.

WAR DIARY
or
INTELLIGENCE SUMMARY.
(Erase heading not required.)

Instructions regarding War Diaries and Intelligence Summaries are contained in F.S. Regs., Part II. and the Staff Manual respectively. Title pages will be prepared in manuscript.

Hour, Date, Place	Summary of Events and Information	Remarks and references to Appendices
March 25th 1915 Hd. Qu. 27th Divisional R.E. RENINGHELST	Capt. J.H. Blair returned from temporary attachment to 3rd Corps and was posted to 2nd Wessex Field Co. R.E. Lieut. G. Moon returned from temporary duty with the 2nd Corps and rejoined his unit (2nd Wessex Fd. Co.) 2nd Wessex engaged all night superintending infantry working parties on G.H.Q. line near DICKEBUSCH.	
March 26th 1915 Hd. Qrs. as above	C.R.E. inspected 1st Wessex Fd. Co. at ZEVECOTEN at 8 a.m. Maj. Gen. A.E. Sandbach (C.E. 2nd Army) called & had long interview with C.R.E. 1st Wessex superintended infantry working parties on G.H.Q. line at night.	
March 27th 1915 Hd. Qrs. as above	C.E. Fifth Corps called with reference to work on G.H.Q. line. Hutting at Canada lines near DICKEBUSCH continued, & new huts completed. 2nd Wessex on G.H.Q. line at night.	
March 28th 1915 Hd. Qrs. as above	C.E. Fifth Corps called with reference to G.H.Q. line. C.R.E. left with him to inspect new line. Lieut. in YPRES arranging details for new R.E. depôt at St. Claypin School. Rue des Chiens. C.R.E. began a new line in open near 1st Wessex continued work on G.H.Q. line at night.	

Army Form C. 2118.

WAR DIARY
or
INTELLIGENCE SUMMARY.
(Erase heading not required.)

Instructions regarding War Diaries and Intelligence Summaries are contained in F.S. Regs., Part II and the Staff Manual respectively. Title pages will be prepared in manuscript.

Hour, Date, Place	Summary of Events and Information	Remarks and references to Appendices
March 29th 1915. Hd. Qrs. 27th Divl. R.E. RENINGHELST	Hutting at Canada Inn near DICKEBUSCH continued with civilian labour. Completed 8 new huts completed. Bulk of R.E. stores removed from R.E. Park DICKEBUSCH to new depot at YPRES. C.R.E. again inspected G.H.Q. Line. 2nd beaver continued work on this line at night.	
March 30th 1915. Hd. Qrs. as above	C.R.E. engaged siting & laying out new 3rd line with Capt. Shannon R.E. R.E. Officers engaged in instructing Officers and men of 81st and 82nd Brigades in sapping and wiring. 1st beaver continued work on G.H.Q. Line at night. Two new huts completed at Canada Inn.	
March 31st 1915. Hd. Qrs. as above	2/Lieut. Calvert and his mining section left RENINGHELST to join 17th Coy R.E. at YPRES. C.R.E. gave lecture to Infantry Officers on Field Defences at 12 o'clk. R.E. Officers continued instructional classes with 81st & 82nd Brigades. 2nd beaver continued work on G.H.Q. Line at night.	
April 1st 1915. Hd. Qrs. as above	C.R.E. continued lecture to Infantry Officers on Field Defences. Two new Officers huts completed at Canada Inn. R.E. Officers continued Instruction of Officers & men of 81st & 82nd Infantry Brigades. 1st beaver on G.H.Q. line at night.	

Army Form C. 2118.

WAR DIARY
or
INTELLIGENCE SUMMARY.
(Erase heading not required.)

Instructions regarding War Diaries and Intelligence Summaries are contained in F. S. Regs., Part II and the Staff Manual respectively. Title pages will be prepared in manuscript.

Hour, Date, Place	Summary of Events and Information	Remarks and references to Appendices
April 2nd 1915 Hd. Qrs. 27th Div'l R.E. RENINGHELST	C.R.E. at YPRES obtaining necessary information with reference to mines, etc. in new area, and analysing as to time required for new line to be taken over by 27th Divn. R.E. from the Field. Major C.E.P. Sankey R.E. was attached to 1st Sussex Field Co to command from 2nd inst. vice Major R.R. Dopler sick. R.E. Stores at REVECOTEN Depot removed to YPRES.	
April 3rd 1915 Hd. Qrs. as before	C.R.E. against YPRES interviewing French Military Authorities re trenches, mines, etc. and making further arrangements in connection with R.E. Stores. Balance of R.E. Stores removed from DIKKEBUSCH to YPRES. Major D.G. Fry left on leave to England.	

Army Form C. 2118.

WAR DIARY
or
INTELLIGENCE SUMMARY.
(Erase heading not required.)

Instructions regarding War Diaries and Intelligence Summaries are contained in F.S. Regs., Part II and the Staff Manual respectively. Title pages will be prepared in manuscript.

Hour, Date, Place	Summary of Events and Information	Remarks and references to Appendices
1915 April 3.	C.R.E. again at YPRES interviewing French military authorities with regard to trenches, mines &c. to be taken over by 27th Division & arranging for R.E. Bat at ST. ALOYSIUS School, RUE DES CHIENS. Further wires received from BIGNEBUSCH to YPRES. Major Fry left for England on leave.	
" 4	C.R.E. at POPERINGHE to meet Major Norton Griffiths with reference to new mining Company. 1st Western Field Coy R.E. ZEVECOTEN for billet at YPRES at 5.30 p.m. Engaged matching office posters & preparing for move tomorrow.	
" 5	Moved from RENINGHELST to YPRES. C.R.E.'s Office & billet at 3 Rue de Carbon near MENIN GATE. Major Norton Griffiths pushed near to confer with C.R.E. at re organization of Mining Co. C.R.E. saw G.O.C. at POTIJZE.	
" 6	C.R.E. assisting Major Griffiths in organising Mining Co. Selecting site for new explosive store in cellar, Rue Granghel Rue du Carbon & making same bomb & splinter proof.	
" 7	C.R.E. visits G.O.C. at POTIJZE daily. Moved explosives to new magazine. 62 men from various Battalions in the Division joined mining Company. Rations & billets arranged. Lt. Evans K.S.L.I. joined unit to take charge of mining Co.	
" 8	Assisting Major Norton Griffiths in arranging work for & organising Mining Co. Posted 10 men to unit.	
" 9	Capt. Kellerby joined Mining Co. also 16 men from R.I.F. 2 from Royal Scots & 38 from Chatham under Lieut Campbell. Major Gen. Landheed called & saw C.R.E.	
" 10	C.R.E. made a reconnaissance of R & R. Bat. with G.S.O. 2. Field Gen. Crudlowsh to by Sapper Lane N. of 17 M. to C.R.E. As being about without leave. Resident Capt. Madox Surrey Yeomanry, Members of Field Staff, Cyclist Co's & Prest Tank R.E.	

(73989) W4141—463. 400,000. 9/14. H.&J.Ltd. Forms/C. 2118/10.

Army Form C. 2118.

WAR DIARY
or
INTELLIGENCE SUMMARY.
(Erase heading not required.)

Instructions regarding War Diaries and Intelligence Summaries are contained in F.S. Regs., Part II. and the Staff Manual respectively. Title pages will be prepared in manuscript.

Hour, Date, Place	Summary of Events and Information	Remarks and references to Appendices
1915 April 11.	Stocktaking in R.E. Park & making arrangements for further material, particularly timber which we have great difficulty in obtaining.	
" 12.	C.R.E. again visited trenches & selected position for supporting south.	
" 13.	Instructing mining officers in explosives. Two enemy officers in R.E. Park. Mining officer reported that in trench 21 they had bored through into space & it was felt they had gone into German trench or mine. It was therefore decided to blow lead in. C.R.E. with Capt Karner & party of Sappers went out at 12 midnight, prepared charge into the perpendicular & fired same electrically in early morning. Explosion successful but few yards about of German trench. Enemy parapet did not appear to be very much damaged.	
" 15	C.R.E. investigated report as to wireless telegraph going on in YPRES. Learned to stand by in event of second attack which was anticipated. Orders given & all arrangements made with Field Companies.	
" 16	Removing R.E. stores to new depot East of MENIN GATE.	
" 17	Continued removal of stores & material to new depot. C.R.E. at BOEZINGHE re timber which we still have difficulty in obtaining. C.E. 5th Corps gave instructions with regard to pontoon bridges to be built over moat S. of MENIN GATE. Made reconnaissance of same.	
" 18	C.R.E. visited Field Companies & inspected work recently carried out in front of 2nd line trenches. YPRES shelled in the evening.	
" 19	Serg. Major Stocker, Major Sanders & Lieut. Manning slightly wounded by splinters during shelling of YPRES by enemy which continued the greater part of the day.	

(73989) W4141—463. 400,000. 9/14. H.&J.Ltd. Forms/C. 2118/16. of the day.

WAR DIARY
or
INTELLIGENCE SUMMARY.
(Erase heading not required.)

Army Form C. 2118.

Instructions regarding War Diaries and Intelligence Summaries are contained in F.S. Regs., Part II. and the Staff Manual respectively. Title pages will be prepared in manuscript.

Hour, Date, Place	Summary of Events and Information	Remarks and references to Appendices
1915 April 20th	C.E. 5th Corps called, inspected R.E. Park & discussed supply of material. Captn. Johnstone R.E. & Capt. Hepburn brought Hardy bored for mining & explained its use. A trial was afterwards made. YPRES heavily shelled throughout day. Much damage done.	
1915 April 21st	C.R.E. at advanced H.Q. Hqrs. POTIJZE. Great difficulty experienced in obtaining sufficient tools & grenades to supply Brigade requirements. Rifle shelling in morning but afterwards quiet. Moved Hd. Qrs. to cellar at No. 5 Rue Van Corbeek.	
" 22nd "	C.E. 2nd Army called & saw Mining Officer. Arrangements made with O./C. R.E. Park STRATEELE for extra supply of sandbags to meet requirements of the Division. Severe bombardment of YPRES started at 5:30 p.m. & continued throughout night. Town practically deserted. Big fires started in many places. These we endeavoured to extinguish but unsuccessful & we were obliged to withdraw our men owing to the heavy shelling.	
" 23rd "	2nd Censor listened to place WEILTJE in a state of defence. Left 2:30 a.m. Shelling of town continued throughout the day. Moved Hd. Qrs. to cellar recently occupied by Admin. Produce Staff of 5th Divn. near MENIN GATE. C.R.E. took G.O.C. of POTIJZE where he spent the night.	
" 24 "	C.R.E. at POTIJZE all day. At 7.0 a.m. 17" shell landed in garden 50 yds from our cellar. Moved Hd. Qrs. to bivouacs & shortly afterwards all billets heavily shelled & buildings wrecked. Shelling continued all day. MENIN GATE still intact & kept open for traffic.	

Army Form C. 2118.

WAR DIARY
or
INTELLIGENCE SUMMARY.
(Erase heading not required.)

Instructions regarding War Diaries and Intelligence Summaries are contained in F. S. Regs., Part II. and the Staff Manual respectively. Title pages will be prepared in manuscript.

Hour, Date, Place		Summary of Events and Information	Remarks and references to Appendices
25.4.15.	3.0.p.m.	Capt. N.D. Noble arrived and took over duties as Adjutant. Capt. S.L. Harvey reported to 1st Wessex Field Co. Commenced removal of explosives from Magazine near MENIN-GATE to 17th Co. R.E. dug-out at Potijze. Completed by evening. H.Qrs. R.E. moved from YPRES to VLAMERTINGHE, CRE remaining with G.O.C. at POTIJZE. Surg-Major Stocker took up quarters with 2nd Wessex Fd Co RE	
26.4.15.	7.0.a.m.	Established 27th Div. RE Park at railway siding, VLAMERTINGHE. Adjutant visited CRE and arranged that Brigades should draw RE Stores from 17Co. RE. YPRES road crowded with reinforcements.	
27.4.15.	2.45.p.m.	VLAMERTINGHE shelled. Billet damaged. HdQrs moved to railway siding near RE Park. Maj R.B Dutton returned from sick leave to 1st Wessex F.C. Maj. Gen Sandbach visited Park and arranged for supply of	
28.4.15.	11.0.a.m	French Wire which was urgently required. VLAMERTINGHE again shelled. Maj Sankey working with 2nd Wessex Field Co. Impossible to meet demands for Very Pistol Ammunition. Ammn. Col. replied they were sending us all they got	
29.4.15.		about 2 men killed and 13 wounded	
30.4.15.		Capt S.L Harvey rejoined 1st Wessex Field Co R.E.	

for CRE 27 Div — April 1915

Horseguards.
7.3.25

My dear Edmonds.

In reply to your letter of 6th—

1. RE work.

When I took over from the French as CRE 27th Div on the line from Hill 60 to the Menin Road, they told me that the only Engineer problem was Mining. This I found to be the case & as we had no mining units I had a great deal of trouble. We did what we could & the situation was really saved by the energy of Sir John Norton Griffiths & the way he chased miners & mining officers up to me — Not only did he do this but he came himself & set the men to work in the line as a mining officer at the places I indicated. He was a wonder & never got the credit he deserved. The trench work was not difficult

2

until we had to draw back & dig a Chord line through Hooge - Frezenburg. Then the difficulty was time & time only. I mean time as compared with the men available to work for we were in a tight place from a fighting point of view.

2. Stores. We had as far as I remember enough R.E. stores & tools. As the Parks had begun to function tho' I still had to buy things locally. Between the two sources I did pretty well. It was quite a different situation in this respect to the 1st Battle when we had NOTHING! Transport for stores was a difficulty but it was overcome —

3. The "G.H.Q." line on 22° April 15 ran through Shell Fire Corner or just in front of it to Zillebeke

on the right & Potonze on the left. It was I think a 3'x 3' trench - traversed & well wired. Nothing more no dug outs nor support or communication trenches. It was a bug bear to the G.S. & I often heard Snow say "Damn the P.H.Q. line", as the wire cut the area into two parts.

4 I believe we made a hideous & bloody mistake in coming back from our original line, through the Herentage Chateau woods, to the line we made in such a hurry through Hooge — It was ordered by P.H.Q. who did not know the ground & who were in a blue funk to put it mildly. I am sure throughout this war was in such an ill managed affray as the 2nd Battle of Ypres.

Whose fault it was God knows, but I expect he will visit it on someone when the Great Assize takes place.

5. <u>Bridges</u>. I don't recognise torn fyins. The only one I had to do with was a Pontoon bridge I (27th D'n RE) put down over the moat, just South of the Menin Gate Causeway or bridge.
It was intended as a relief bridge but curiously enough it was more shelled than the permanent bridge — It was approached by an old Sally Port through the ramparts. I had a lot of trouble keeping it alive & lost most of my pontoons by fire & other things in doing so —

6. I am reading Liam Vol II

with great interest — Its extraordinarily
accurate I think + produces
reasons for many things that none of
us understood at the time.

There is one thing you mention but
don't elaborate vizt. the incident
of the Herintier Stable — It impressed
me very much because, in the light
of later events, it appeared that
we wasted a lot of energy over it.
I pressed personally to have it
retaken + I got it done, but the
French when they took over did not
worry when they found we had just
lost the place for a second time!

Yours sincerely
J Wallen

Army Form C. 2118.

WAR DIARY
or
INTELLIGENCE SUMMARY.
(Erase heading not required.)

Instructions regarding War Diaries and Intelligence Summaries are contained in F.S. Regs., Part II. and the Staff Manual respectively. Title pages will be prepared in manuscript.

Hour, Date, Place	Summary of Events and Information	Remarks and references to Appendices
1.6.15.	2/Lieut T.S. Bliss admitted to Hospital. VLAMERTINGHE shelled. Also YPRES road near Park. No damage to Park. Coo. reported one man wounded.	
2.6.15.	Brought back all valuable stores from old Park at YPRES to VLAMERTINGHE.	
3.6.15.	SURG. MAJ. STOCKER returned to H.Q. from 2nd Wessex Field Co. Major C.E.P. Sankey slightly wounded. and 1 man killed (w.m)	
4.6.15.	Attempted to bring back explosives from HOOGE, but unable to complete owing to heavy shell fire. Lieut C.E.R. Pottinger reported severely wounded. 3 men wounded. C.R.E. returned from POTIJZE to Advanced Signal Centre. (w.m)	
5.6.15.	H.Q. moved and joined 27th Division H.Q. Work on Reserve "Dug-outs" for Brigadiers. Major C.E.P. Sankey admitted Hospital. 3 men wounded. Company H.Q. moved to safer positions in rear. Experience in Companies sent urgents demands to replace casualties and reinforcements very slow in arriving.	
6.6.15.	The Wessex Field Co. very short, and reinforcements very slow in arriving, from Coo. reported 3 men killed and 5 wounded. Lieut R.B. Pitt, 1st Wessex temporarily attached to 2nd Wessex Field Co.	
7.6.15.	who were very short of Officers & N.C.O.s & men. Conference re. G.H.Q. line. Maj. Singer, O.C. 14th Co., put in charge of it. Co. reported 1 man wounded. Construction of Supporting Points behind front line ordered. (w.m)	

Army Form C. 2118.

WAR DIARY
or
INTELLIGENCE SUMMARY.
(Erase heading not required.)

Instructions regarding War Diaries and Intelligence Summaries are contained in F.S. Regs., Part II. and the Staff Manual respectively. Title pages will be prepared in manuscript.

Hour, Date, Place	Summary of Events and Information	Remarks and references to Appendices
8.5.15.	Work on "dug-out" for G.O.C. R.A. H.Qrs. & Coys. standing by ready to move at a moment's notice. Heavy fighting. Cos. reported 2 men wounded.	
9.5.15.	Reconnaissance of MENIN GATE CAUSEWAY with a view to demolition. Repairing Pontoon Bridge near MENIN GATE, destroyed by shell fire. Reconnaissance of Canal bridges with a view to demolition. 17th Co. R.E. put in charge S. of YPRES. H.Qrs and Cos. standing by. Positions of Cos. in case of retirement discussed. Preparation of two land mines. Lieut CER Pottinger recommended for Russian Decoration. Cos. reported one man wounded.	YSM.
10.5.15.	CRE inspected GHQ Line. 2nd Lieut PA Coombe joined 17th Co. as reinforcement. 2nd Lieut L.C. Chasey wounded.	Yr.
11.5.15.	Clearing roadway at MENIN GATE. Arranged to issue R.E. Stores to 1st & 2nd Cavalry Divisions. 2nd Lieut S. Maurice seriously wounded & died of wounds. Cos. reported 2 men killed and 7 wounded. 2nd Lieut Hall slightly wounded.	YSM.
12.5.15.	Preparing Supporting Points for occupation. Shortage of explosives, owing to large demands of 171 Mining Co. Cos reported 2 men killed & 8 wounded.	YSM.

Army Form C. 2118.

WAR DIARY
or
INTELLIGENCE SUMMARY.
(Erase heading not required.)

Instructions regarding War Diaries and Intelligence Summaries are contained in F. S. Regs., Part II. and the Staff Manual respectively. Title pages will be prepared in manuscript.

Hour, Date, Place	Summary of Events and Information	Remarks and references to Appendices
13.5.15.	Mining Party urgently required in 82 Brigade. Not possible to get them up before daylight. Recive Pontoon Equipment in YPRES destroyed by shell-fire. Draft of 34 men arrived as reinforcement for 17 Co. Lieut. G. Moon admitted Hospital after being gassed. WSM	
14.5.15.	4 Officers reported as reinforcement for 171 Mining Co. Closing road and railway on G.H.Q. Line. Cos. reported one man killed and one wounded. WSM	
15.5.15.	Maj. C.E.P.Sankey reported & was put in Charge of GHQ Line & Switches. Lieut G.C.Schutz joined 2nd Wessex F.Co. Cos. reported 7 men wounded. WSM	
16.5.15.	Miner urgently required in SANCTUARY WOOD. Reconnaissance by Capt WELLESLEY. No casualties reported	
17.5.15.	Lieut T.S. Blow returned from Hospital. Point of junction with 5th Div. on ZILLEBEKE Switch not clear and fixed after reference to C.E. WSM 2 men reported wounded.	
18.5.15.	Lieut. Pitt rejoined 1st Wessex after temporary attachment to 2nd Wessex 17 Co. and 1st Wessex to come under orders of Cavalry Corps from 6.0 a.m. 19th. 2nd Wessex to remain with 82 Brigade, assisted by one Section 1st Wessex, if required. WSM	

Army Form C. 2118.

WAR DIARY
or
INTELLIGENCE SUMMARY.
(Erase heading not required.)

Instructions regarding War Diaries and Intelligence Summaries are contained in F. S. Regs., Part II and the Staff Manual respectively. Title pages will be prepared in manuscript.

Hour, Date, Place	Summary of Events and Information	Remarks and references to Appendices
18.5.15.	Handing over details to CRE Cavalry Corps. 2nd Brigade ~~H.Q.~~ moved back to Etaminet on POPERINGHE – RENINGHELST Road. CRE remained with GOC till change of command completed.	
19.5.15.	No casualties reported. WM 82 Brigade concerning about Engineer Work, owing to length of line held under Cavalry Corps. Maj. Sankey still in charge of G.H.Q. Line. 2 men reported wounded. WM CRE rejoined HQ 6".	
20.5.15.	Coss putting Equipment in order and concentrating transport ready for use. No casualties reported. WM	
21.5.15.	CRE proceeded on Leave. 2nd Wessex to be accommodate whole Company in present "dug-outs" in view of shortage of accommodation. 2 men reported wounded. WM	
22.5.15.	Arranged with DADOS to deliver to RE direct by A.O.D. Lorry, for the time being, owing to shortage of transport. One man reported wounded. WM	
23.5.15.	All trench mortars without enlarged chambers to be returned to A.O.D. for alteration. One man reported wounded. WM	

Army Form C. 2118.

WAR DIARY
or
INTELLIGENCE SUMMARY.
(Erase heading not required.)

Instructions regarding War Diaries and Intelligence Summaries are contained in F. S. Regs., Part II and the Staff Manual respectively. Title pages will be prepared in manuscript.

Hour, Date, Place	Summary of Events and Information	Remarks and references to Appendices
24.5.15.	One man reported wounded.	WR
25.5.15.	Reported that "Mills" hand-grenade much superior to other patterns. Supply of bombs still insufficient to meet requirements. No casualties reported.	WR
26.5.15.	3 men reported wounded. Division ordered to move to relieve 6th Division. Companies ordered to be in readiness to move.	WR
27.5.15	Capt W Jenkins joined 2nd Wessex. Lieut W P Jones joined 1st Wessex. [2nd Wessex moved to relieve 12th Co. R.E.] CRE returned from leave.	WR
28.5.15.	One man reported wounded. G.O.C. expressed warm appreciation of work done by R.E. Maj. Sankey at disposal of C.E. 3rd Corps. CRE and Adjutant visited 6th Division and 2nd Wessex, who had already relieved 12th Co. R.E.	WR
29.5.15.	Establishing Divisional Park at Armentières.	WR
30.5.15.	Work on Subsidiary Line to be arranged & supervised by H.Q. 6th. Disposal of Civilian Working Parties.	WR
31.5.15.	R.S.M. reported sick and admitted Hospital. H.Qrs moved to CROIX DU BAC. Taking over from CRE 6th Division.	WR

C.R.E.,
    27th Division.

    The Major General Commanding the Division wishes all ranks of the Royal Engineers (Regular + Territorial) under your Command informed how much he appreciates the splendid and arduous work which under your guidance they have performed during the trying 5 weeks through which the Division has just passed. The grit and valour displayed by all who have borne an equal part with the artillery and infantry in fighting, and at the same time have had to undergo a test of endurance perhaps greater then any other arm engaged reflects the greatest credit on all concerned. You, your officers, N.C.O.s and men must be proud in the knowledge that they have upheld and even added to the glorious records of the Corps of Royal Engineers.

                                                      H. L. Reed.

28th May, 1915.   Lieut. Col., G.S.,
                                                  27th Division.

121/5585

27th Division

H.d.Q.rs R.E. 27th Division

Vol II 1 — 30.6.15.

Confidential

War Diary

of

27th Divisional Engineers

Headquarters

From 1st June 1915

To 30th June 1915

Army Form C. 2118.

WAR DIARY
or
INTELLIGENCE SUMMARY.
(Erase heading not required.)

Instructions regarding War Diaries and Intelligence Summaries are contained in F.S. Regs., Part II and the Staff Manual respectively. Title pages will be prepared in manuscript.

Hour, Date, Place	Summary of Events and Information	Remarks and references to Appendices
1.6.15.	Lieut. N. Harbutt reported Hospital sick. Detachment 20th Co. R.E. temporarily placed under orders of C.R.E. 27th Div. Civilian Gang for work at R.E. Park taken on for making hurdles, gun pits for Subsidiary Line, and perhaps for other requirements for Brigades. Arrangements for removal of timber from Railway Annexe and for issue from R.E. Woodyard, RUE DE FLANDRES. Orders by C.R.E. as to demolition of bridges in case of retirement. 1st Wessex to take ERQUINGHEM and PONT DE NIEPPE, Detachment 2/ Wessex HOUPLINES Bridge & sluices. Bridging Train BAC ST MAUR, 17 Co. LE BIZET Bridges, and 2nd Wessex HOUPLINES Bridge & sluices.	
2.6.15.	Adjutant rejoined Hd Qrs after being at R.E. Park since 29.5.15. Shortage in supply of Grenades noticed. C.R.E. visited sight of 82 T.B. line. C.R.E. and Adjt visited Subsidiary Line & Supporting Points at TOUQUET. Coo. reported 1 man wounded.	
3.6.15.	Inspection of Subsidiary Line at BOIS-GRENIER. G.O.C. 3rd Corps visited bomb-shops in 27th Div. & found satisfactory. Arranged to lend timber to Cos. of 9th Division on requisition by C.R.E. 9th Division.	

(73989) W4141—463. 400,000. 9/14. H.&J.Ltd. Forms/C. 2118/10.

WAR DIARY
or
INTELLIGENCE SUMMARY.
(Erase heading not required.)

Army Form C. 2118.

Hour, Date, Place	Summary of Events and Information	Remarks and references to Appendices
4.6.15.	Inspection of Subsidiary line at CHAPELLE D'ARMENTIERES. Decision that Cos. should superintend all work in front of Subsidiary line. Huts for accommodation of Signal Co. ordered. Proto-oxygen School installed in ARMENTIERES.	
5.6.15.	Organising civilian gangs for work on Subsidiary line. Organising transport for issue of RE Stores to Brigades & RE Cos daily. CRE & Adjt visited works at TOURVET. Interpreter R Brason reported for duty.	
6.6.15.	APM reviewed all civilian gangs at RE Park. Supervisors for civilian gangs reported at RE Park for duty. Reinforcement of 26 men arrived for 17th Co.	
7.6.15.	Adjutant pointed out work on Subsidiary line to Supervisors. CRE & Adjt visited works at HOUPLINES.	
8.6.15.	Civilian gangs started work at BOIS-GRENIER, CHAPELLE D'ARMENTIERES, & TOURVET. Reinforcement of 5 men joined 2nd Wessex Co.	
9.6.15.	Inspection of work on Subsidiary Line. New Gang started at CHAPELLE Cemetery. Organisation of 2nd Bridging Train Transport to take up materials by night for work on Subsidiary line.	

WAR DIARY
or
INTELLIGENCE SUMMARY.
(Erase heading not required.)

Army Form C. 2118.

Hour, Date, Place	Summary of Events and Information	Remarks and references to Appendices
10.6.15.	Inspection of work on Subsidiary Line by Field Co. 12th Divn attached for instruction to 17th Co till 16th inst. L./Cpl. Bellinger appointed Engineer Clerk, authority DAG. Base. Co. reported one man died of wounds. WSN	
11.6.15.	CRE visited 19 I.B. Line. Inspection of work on Subsidiary Line. Brushwood required by Co., CE 3rd Corps asked for supply. WSN	
12.6.15.	CRE visited 82 I.B. Line. Inspection of work on Subsidiary Line, and of existing works at HOUPLINES. Shortage in supply of timber apparent. Enquiries made, found that last consignment not arrived as scheduled. WSN	
13.6.15.	Germans blew up mine at TOUQUET, demolishing house in our lines and burying 2 miners. No other damage. Inspection of work on Subsidiary Line & of the ground round Le RUAGE for a Supporting Point behind. WSN	
14.6.15.	G.S. asked for a decision as to extension of Subsidiary Line N of road, and to include large sand dune farm S. of road. Also proposal to fill up or straighten out communication trenches. Inspection of work on Subsidiary Line. Scheme for demolition of ERQUINGHEM Bridge discussed, & decided to keep charges & leads in dug-out near bridge. WSN	

WAR DIARY
or
INTELLIGENCE SUMMARY.
(Erase heading not required.)

Army Form C. 2118.

Instructions regarding War Diaries and Intelligence Summaries are contained in F.S. Regs., Part II and the Staff Manual respectively. Title pages will be prepared in manuscript.

Hour, Date, Place	Summary of Events and Information	Remarks and references to Appendices
15.6.15.	87th Field Co., 12th Div, attached for instruction to 17th Co. Inspection of work on Subsidiary Line. Decision by G.S. to carry out all the proposed alterations to the line near LE RUAGE. Evidence of German mining activity at FRELINGHIEN. British Camouflet fired at TOUQUET.	Esri.
16.6.15.	81 I.B. report mining suspected near LILLE road. Shaft sunk & listening carried out without result. Inspection of work on Subsidiary Line. Pointing out & explaining work at LE RUAGE to subordinates. Formation of civilian gang for work at LE RUAGE. 2Lieut C.A. Coombes reported wounded. One man wounded.	Esri.
17.6.15.	Scheme for demolition of BAC ST MAUR bridge discussed, decided to add charge in centre pier, & to keep charges & leads in dug-out near bridge. Orders to readjust slightly lines held by 80, 81st, 262nd Brigades. One man reported wounded.	Esri.

WAR DIARY
or
INTELLIGENCE SUMMARY.

(Erase heading not required.)

Army Form C. 2118.

Instructions regarding War Diaries and Intelligence Summaries are contained in F.S. Regs., Part II. and the Staff Manual respectively. Title pages will be prepared in manuscript.

Hour, Date, Place	Summary of Events and Information	Remarks and references to Appendices
18.6.15.	Inspection of work on Subsidiary Line. Started work at LE RUAGE. Orders to make HOUPLINES CEMETERY strong point V.L. Aspland joined 1st Wessex Field Co.	
7.5 p.m. to 7.30 p.m.	Two series of mines and Camouflet successfully fired at FRELINGHIEN. Houses demolished and much damage to German line. Germans seen retiring from their trenches. Artillery & rifle fire thought to be inadequate; i.e. heavy fire would probably have caused the enemy many casualties. Inspection of work on Subsidiary Line and laying out near work near LE RUAGE.	
19.6.15.		
20.6.15.	Bangalore of Ironworks arrived for distribution to Companies. Inspection of Subsidiary Line at FERME DE BUTERNE. Decided to make a strong point. 2nd Lieut R.A. Williams joined 17th Co.	
21.6.15.	Inspection of Subsidiary line, & laying out work at FERME DE BUTERNE.	

WAR DIARY
or
INTELLIGENCE SUMMARY.
(Erase heading not required.)

Army Form C. 2118.

Instructions regarding War Diaries and Intelligence Summaries are contained in F.S. Regs., Part II and the Staff Manual respectively. Title pages will be prepared in manuscript.

Hour, Date, Place	Summary of Events and Information	Remarks and references to Appendices
22.6.15.	Inspection of extending line. Decided not to clear crops more than necessary till work nearing completion. Crops mostly unsown and of small value. One man reported wounded.	EWR
23.6.15.	Inspection of work on Subsidiary Line. Arranged to hand over line N. of LYS to CRE 12th Divn. Discussion re provision of additional wells in case of water-famine.	EWR
24.6.15.	Inspection of work on Subsidiary Line. C.E. decided that normal wages of workmen should be 3 francs for 7 hour work, 4 francs by night. One man reported killed, 174th Mining Co.	EWR
25.6.15.	Inspection of work on Subsidiary Line. Fresh orders issued as to payment of civilians, keeping of Cards and Time Sheets, & preparation of Pay Sheets. Divisional Operation Order received, detailing moves for readjustment of line on night 27th - 28th - Line N. of LYS to be handed over to 12th Divn. 2 men reported wounded.	EWR
26.6.15.	Inspection of work on Subsidiary Line. Germans exploded mine near FRELINGHIEN trx from our trenches. Explosion to our trenches. Discussion re surface drainage during winter months.	EWR

Army Form C. 2118.

WAR DIARY
or
INTELLIGENCE SUMMARY.
(Erase heading not required.)

Instructions regarding War Diaries and Intelligence Summaries are contained in F.S. Regs., Part II. and the Staff Manual respectively. Title pages will be prepared in manuscript.

Hour, Date, Place	Summary of Events and Information	Remarks and references to Appendices
27.6.15.	Inspection of work on Subsidiary Line. Formation of Brigade Bombing Schools & issue of bombs. Supply to Brigades likely to be seriously affected. Pointed out to G.S. Discussion with O.C. of Cos as to disposal of surface water & drainage generally, and also as to pattern of dug-outs in Supporting Line. Readjustment of line as detailed in Div. Operation Order No 50.	
28.6.15.	Inspection of work on Subsidiary Line. C.E. visited disused "dug outs" in Support line & water supply. Shortage of pitprops pitprop mine near WEZ MACQUART inside they own lines, asked to restrict wires of timber except for defence purposes. One man wounded. Discussion as to stocks of Grenades to be held by Brigades and R.E. Park. Decision to equalize & slightly decrease Brigade Stocks.	
29.6.15.	Inspection of work on Subsidiary Line. Laying out new line at HOUPLINES Cemetery. One man wounded 28th died of wounds. Discussion at 3rd Corps H.Q. OP.29 as to type of Machine Gun Emplacement. Discussion with O.C. 174 Co as to proposed mine near LILLE road.	
30.6.15.	Inspection of Subsidiary Line. Work commenced at HOUPLINES Cemetery. Trials for pattern of concealed and blinded Machine Gun Emplacement. Discussion as to pattern of pump required (a) for drawing from deep wells in summer (b) for trench work in winter. Div. Order that no timber to be issued without counter-signature of R.E. Officer. Design for shelters etc to be submitted. One man reported wounded.	

Walker Lt Col
O.C. 27th Division
1.7.15

(73989) W4141—463. 400,000. 9/14. H.&J.Ltd. Forms/C. 2118/10.

27th Division.

121/6357

HQ 27th RE. 27th Division

Vol III

Confidential

War Diary.

of

Headquarters 27th Divisional R.E.
From 1st July 1915 - to 31st July 1915.

Lot. Col.
C.R.E. 27th Division.

Army Form C. 2118.

WAR DIARY
or
INTELLIGENCE SUMMARY.
(Erase heading not required.)

Instructions regarding War Diaries and Intelligence Summaries are contained in F.S. Regs., Part II. and the Staff Manual respectively. Title pages will be prepared in manuscript.

Hour, Date, Place	Summary of Events and Information	Remarks and references to Appendices
1.7.15. 6.0 a.m.	Inspection of work on Subsidiary Line at LE RUAGE, HOUPLINES Cemetery, and FERME DE BUTERNE.	Fish.
3.0 p.m.	Inspection of Subsidiary Line. Siting of Machine Gun Emp to	
6.0 p.m.	Arranged to obtain Brushwood Pickets from LA MOTTE AU BOIS, owing to shortage of Timber.	
2.7.15 6 a.m.	Visited Subsidiary Line. (Adjt went on leave to England). Duties temporary taken over by 2nd C.D. Shelton R.E.(T)	
3.7.15 6 a.m.	Visited Subsidiary Line at LE RUAGE, HOUPLINES Cemetery, and FERME DE BUTERNE with O.C. No 6 M/c GUN BATTERY reference Machine Gun Monnting sites.	
11 a.m.	Conference of C.R.E.s in III Corps with C.E. III Corps at his office. Arrangements made for Stores & materials for different Divisions.	

Army Form C. 2118.

WAR DIARY
or
INTELLIGENCE SUMMARY.
(Erase heading not required.)

Instructions regarding War Diaries and Intelligence Summaries are contained in F.S. Regs., Part II. and the Staff Manual respectively. Title pages will be prepared in manuscript.

Hour, Date, Place		Summary of Events and Information	Remarks and references to Appendices
4.7.15	3 p.m.	O.C. No 6 M/c Gun Battery + C.R.E. visited M/c mountings at Billet of 2nd Wessex Co. R.E.	
	9.30 pm	Trial of rockets. Inspected by G.O.C. 27th Division	
5.7.15	4.30 a.m.	Inspection of work in Subsidiary line at LE RUAGE, HOUPLINES Cemetery & FERME DE BUTERNE	
	10 a.m. 5 p.m.	Visited MERVILLE - ESTAIRES - NIEPPE FOREST for materials available for defences - chiefly timber obtained.	
6.7.15	5 a.m. 6 a.m.	Inspection of Subsidiary line. C.R.E. visited subsidiary line with O.C. No 6 M/c Gun Battery - Selection of suitable M/c sites.	
	2 p.m. 6 p.m.	Visited Field G.S. Visited II Army Workshop reference stores under construction.	

Army Form C. 2118.

WAR DIARY
or
INTELLIGENCE SUMMARY.
(Erase heading not required.)

Instructions regarding War Diaries and Intelligence Summaries are contained in F.S. Regs., Part II and the Staff Manual respectively. Title pages will be prepared in manuscript.

Hour, Date, Place		Summary of Events and Information	Remarks and references to Appendices
7-7-15	5 a.m.	Inspection of work on Subsidiary line for whole length. — O.C.	
	6. a.m.	N/c Gun Battery consulted with G.R.E. for additional M/c gun positions.	
		One civilian wounded on work at HOUPLINE cemetery.	
	11.30 a.m.	Visited Field Coys, visited portion of front line trenches with	
	5.0 p.m.	O.C. 2nd Wessex R.E.	MDS.
		Made new arrangements for issues of timber for Divisions	
8.7.15.	6.0 a.m.	Visited Subsidiary Line.	
		Removed timber from HOUPLINES Yard to R.E. Park, portion to 173rd Mining Company.	for.
9.7.15.	6.0 a.m.	Visited Subsidiary Line. Arrangements to command communication trenches decided on. Yeomanry and Cyclists to provide Working Parties.	for.
10.7.15.	5.30 a.m.	Inspection of Subsidiary Line RUAGE — FERME DE BUTERNE and decided on work to be done by RA Working Parties.	
		2 men reported wounded (one on 9th)	for.
11.7.15.	8.30 a.m.	Reconnaissance of work to be done by RA Working Parties on Subsidiary Line with R.A. Officers.	for.

Army Form C. 2118.

WAR DIARY
or
INTELLIGENCE SUMMARY.
(Erase heading not required.)

Instructions regarding War Diaries and Intelligence Summaries are contained in F.S. Regs., Part II and the Staff Manual respectively. Title pages will be prepared in manuscript.

Hour, Date, Place		Summary of Events and Information	Remarks and references to Appendices
12.7.15.	6.0.a.m.	Inspection of Subsidiary Line and arrangements for R.A. working Parties.	
		Reported to G.S. that Bomb School use up Bombs faster than they are supplied. Decision as to formation of Bomb Factory asked for. Reinforcement 9 men for 17th Co.	WSR
13.7.15.	5.30.a.m.	Inspection of M.G. Emplacements on Subsidiary Line. R.A., Yeomanry and Cyclist Parties at Work.	
	2.0.p.m.	Inspection of Front Line at RUE DU BOIS with CE 3rd Corps. Reinforcement 1 man for 2nd Wessex.	
	9.0.p.m.	Preliminary discussion with A Branch as to new Billeting Arrangements and with G.S. as to reallotment of Field Cos. Two men 174 Co. reported killed on 13th.	WSR
14.7.15.	7.0.a.m.	Reconnoitred for new Billets for Field Cos.	
	10.0 a.m.	Visit from CRE 50th Division re. taking over portion of our line	WSR
15.7.15.	6.30.a.m.	Inspection of Subsidiary Line. Arranged for civilian working parties to work in new positions from 17th.	
	2.30.p.m.	Pointed out work in new positions to civilian supervisors. 82nd Brigade relieved by 12th Division.	WSR

WAR DIARY
or
INTELLIGENCE SUMMARY.
(Erase heading not required.)

Army Form C. 2118.

Instructions regarding War Diaries and Intelligence Summaries are contained in F.S. Regs., Part II. and the Staff Manual respectively. Title pages will be prepared in manuscript.

Hour, Date, Place	Summary of Events and Information	Remarks and references to Appendices
16.7.15. 5.30.a.m	Inspection of Subsidiary Line and arrangements for work on new M.G. Emplacements.	
	2nd Wessex moved to new Billet in Espringham	
3.30 p.m	Inspection of hutting for Reserve Brigade.	fin
	Major Singer O.C. 17 Co. appointed C.R.E 50th Division.	
	Part of 60th I.B. relieved by 50th Division.	
17.7.15. 6.0.a.m	Inspection of Subsidiary Line. Civilian Parties at work in new positions	
	17 Co. in temporary Billet until new Billet at L'ARMÉE vacant.	
2.0 p.m	G.O.C. went into question of supply of Bombs and Very Lights	fin
18.7.15.	G.O.C. inspected Subsidiary Line and ordered another layer of wire entanglement to be erected beyond bombing distance, and wire to be arranged to direct attack onto strongest parts of line	
	Arranged for supply of Huts from 20th Co. R.E.	
	Arranged for Billeting 20th Co. at PETIT MORTIER	fin

WAR DIARY
or
INTELLIGENCE SUMMARY.

(Erase heading not required.)

Army Form C. 2118.

Instructions regarding War Diaries and Intelligence Summaries are contained in F.S. Regs., Part II and the Staff Manual respectively. Title pages will be prepared in manuscript.

Hour, Date, Place	Summary of Events and Information	Remarks and references to Appendices
19.7.15. 6.0.a.m.	Inspected Subsidiary Line, and arranged for G.O.Co instructions re wire entanglements to be carried out. Reconny and Cyclists working on wiring. Shortage of barbed wire. 17th Co moved into Camp Byst near L'ARMÉE. "Dug-out" mops. 2nd Wessex started making cement blocks for dug-out roofs.	JWD
7.0 p.m.	No1 Park asked to send barbed wire and other supply stores by rail. One man 1st Wessex reported wounded on 18th.	JWD
20.7.15. 5.30.a.m.	Inspected Subsidiary Line. Discussion as to Winter Hutting. One man 17th Co accidentally drowned.	JWD
2.0 p.m.		
21.7.15. 6.0.a.m.	Inspected Subsidiary Line. Reconnaissance for communication trenches and supporting points in rear.	JWD
10.0.a.m.	Discussion re Trench Tramways.	
22.7.15. 5.30.a.m.	Inspected Subsidiary Line	
2.30 p.m.	Discussion re Electric & Power for lighting, Pumps etc. Capt. G.A.Picken joined 1st Wessex. Lieut. C.Smith joined 2nd Wessex, both from Base.	JWD

WAR DIARY
or
INTELLIGENCE SUMMARY

(Erase heading not required.)

Army Form C. 2118.

Instructions regarding War Diaries and Intelligence Summaries are contained in F.S. Regs., Part II. and the Staff Manual respectively. Title pages will be prepared in manuscript.

Hour, Date, Place		Summary of Events and Information	Remarks and references to Appendices
23.7.15.	6.0 a.m.	Inspection of Subsidiary Line. Decision to make strong points at railway crossing I.14.b/5, road junction I.20.a.3, PARK ROW communication and Sheffield Avenue. Capt G.A. Pitken reverts to 'dient'.	fwn
24.7.15.	12.30 p.m.	Enclosed work for one Batt⁹ at BOIS GRENIER decided on. Inspection of site with G.S.O.1 and general line decided.	
	3.0 p.m.	General line of Trench Tramways discussed. G.O.C. ordered new Breastwork Support Line and Breastwork Communication Avenues. Major T. Gracey arrived from Base and took over command of 17th Co R.E.YSR	
25.7.15.	2.0 p.m.	Laying out work at BOIS GRENIER. One man 1st Wessex killed	fwn
26.7.15.	5.30 a.m.	Inspection of Subsidiary Line. Wiring Parties stopped for want of barbed wire.	
	2.45 p.m.	Inspection of proposed work at BOIS GRENIER with G.O.C. 80th IB. Types of work decided on and general line approved. Routes of Trench Tramways decided on	fwn

Army Form C. 2118.

WAR DIARY
or
INTELLIGENCE SUMMARY
(Erase heading not required.)

Instructions regarding War Diaries and Intelligence Summaries are contained in F. S. Regs., Part II. and the Staff Manual respectively. Title pages will be prepared in manuscript.

Hour, Date, Place		Summary of Events and Information	Remarks and references to Appendices
27.7.15.	5.30.a.m.	Inspection of Subsidiary Line. Arranged to move tools & materials to Infantry Working Parties.	
	2.30.p.m.	Discussion re type of breastwork for Support Line.	
	8.0.p.m.	80 IB commenced work on supporting point BOIS GRENIER 2 reliefs of 500 men for 4 hours each. Lieut Blair in charge.	fsm
28.7.15.	5.0.a.m.	Inspection of Subsidiary Line & BOIS GRENIER supporting point.	
	9.30.a.m.	Reconnaissance of lines for Trench Tramway.	
	5.0.p.m.	Inspection of work at BOIS GRENIER with GOC 80 IB, & communications inside the work decided.	
		a/RSM Le Marquand arrived & took over duties.	
	8.0.p.m.	80 IB working BOIS GRENIER two 4 hour reliefs of 500 men.	fsm
29.7.15.	5.30.a.m.	Inspection of work BOIS GRENIER and Subsidiary Line	
	2.30.p.m.	Types of work for new Support Line decided on.	
		Reinforcements, 1 man 1st Wessex, 1 man 2nd Wessex, 7 men 1st M.Co arrived.	
	8.0.p.m.	80 IB working BOIS GRENIER two 4 hour reliefs of 500 men	fsm

WAR DIARY
or
INTELLIGENCE SUMMARY.
(Erase heading not required.)

Army Form C. 2118.

Hour, Date, Place	Summary of Events and Information	Remarks and references to Appendices
30 5.30 a.m.	Visited Subsidiary line and work at BOIS GRENIER. Difficulty experienced in supply of material for 1000 4 hour reliefs of Infantry, & for carbon and Yeomanry Parties.	
2.0 p.m.	Visited 1st Army Workshops, BETHUNE, with G.S.O. 1, and arranged for supply of Grenades.	
8.0 p.m.	80 I.B. working BOIS GRENIER. Two 4 hour reliefs of 500 men.	from
31 7.15		
5.30 a.m.	Inspection of M.G. Emplacements Subsidiary line with O.C. M.V.G.S. and of work at BOIS GRENIER.	
5.0 p.m.	Inspection of work at BOIS GRENIER with G.O.C. 80 I.B. Lines of retrenchment decided on.	
8.0 p.m.	80 I.B. working one 4 hour relief of 1000 men.	from

121/6743

27th Division.

HdQrs RE. 27th Division

Vol IV

August 15

CONFIDENTIAL

WAR DIARY

OF

HEADQUARTERS 27TH DIVISIONAL ENGINEERS.

FROM — AUG 1ST 1915   TO — AUG. 31ST 1915.

Army Form C. 2118.

WAR DIARY
or
INTELLIGENCE SUMMARY

(Erase heading not required.)

Instructions regarding War Diaries and Intelligence Summaries are contained in F. S. Regs, Part II. and the Staff Manual respectively. Title pages will be prepared in manuscript.

Hour, Date, Place		Summary of Events and Information	Remarks and references to Appendices
1.8.15.	7.0. a.m.	Laying out retrenchments and Internal Communications BOIS GRENIER	
	3.0. p.m.	Visited No 1 RE Park & arranged for supply of same.	
	4.0 p.m.	G.O.C. inspected Support Line.	Eson
2.8.15.	5.30. a.m.	Inspected Subsidiary Line & MG Emplacements with O.C. M.M.G.S.	
	11.30. a.m.	Discussion re Horse Standings	
		4 Infantry officers attached to 176 RE for instruction.	Eson
3.8.15.	5.30. a.m.	Inspected Subsidiary Line.	
		84th Field Co started work with 17th Co for instruction.	
	1.30. p.m.	Visited ISBERGUES re steel plates and Muzzle Pivot MG Mountings. Impossible to obtain. Visited LILLERS same purpose.	
		1 Scout Pigott joined 1st Wessex Field Co.	
		Inspected Subsidiary Line.	Eson
4.8.15.	6.30. a.m.		
	1.30 p.m.	Visited Neuville re manufacture of sludge pumps, periscopes etc, and purchase of Canvas for Huts.	Eson

Army Form C. 2118.

WAR DIARY
or
INTELLIGENCE SUMMARY
(Erase heading not required.)

Instructions regarding War Diaries and Intelligence Summaries are contained in F.S. Regs, Part II. and the Staff Manual respectively. Title pages will be prepared in manuscript.

Hour, Date, Place		Summary of Events and Information	Remarks and references to Appendices
5.8.15.	6.0 a.m.	Visited Subsidiary Line	
	2.30 p.m.	Visited LILLERS re M.G. mounting, N°1 REP shop, and ISBERGUES re purchase of steel rods & L iron for steel pickets.	ESn
6.8.15	5.30 a.m.	Visited Subsidiary Line. Drainage trenches & cleaning country drains	
	11.0 a.m.	G.O.C. visited Subsidiary line and decided positions of Gaps to be left for counter attack.	ESn
7.8.15.	6.0 a.m.	Visited Subsidiary Line. Work on Gaps ordered.	
	9.0 a.m.	Discussion re pattern of M.G. platform to be adopted.	
	12. noon	C.E. visited to discuss possibilities of use of Electric pumps & drainage	ESn

1247 W 3299 200,000 (E) 8/14 J.B.C. & A. Forms/C. 2118/11.

Army Form C. 2118.

WAR DIARY
or
INTELLIGENCE SUMMARY

(Erase heading not required.)

Instructions regarding War Diaries and Intelligence Summaries are contained in F.S. Regs., Part II. and the Staff Manual respectively. Title pages will be prepared in manuscript.

Hour, Date, Place	Summary of Events and Information	Remarks and references to Appendices
8.8.15. 6.30 a.m.	Visited Subsidiary Line. Repairing damage done by H.M. Damaged slight run.	
10.0 a.m.	CE 3rd Corps visited & discussed demolition of Bridges.	
2.0 p.m.	Visited ISBERGUES and placed order for 1000 steel Entanglement pickets and 70 tons steel rails & Girders for Dug-outs. Visited 8th Railway Co. re M.G. Mountings. Visited CRE 20th Division and arranged about allotments of Timber and Stores.	ISn
9.8.15. 6.30 a.m.	Visited Subsidiary Line. Disposal of surface water. Repairing slight damage done by direct hit of 5.9" shell. Capt MCM Who joined 2nd Wessex Field Co. for duty	ISn
10.8.15 6.0 a.m.	Visited Subsidiary Line & work on Support Line. Wooden wire entanglement pickets in front of Front Line rotten in some places; I men ordered to replace them as far as possible. Shortage of wire netting, much used for revetting, & for telephone lines for RA. Impossible to purchase anywhere. Det 111th Railway Co. attached to 17th Field Company for laying of Trench Tramways.	ISn

Army Form C. 2118.

WAR DIARY
or
INTELLIGENCE SUMMARY

(Erase heading not required.)

Instructions regarding War Diaries and Intelligence Summaries are contained in F. S. Regs., Part II. and the Staff Manual respectively. Title pages will be prepared in manuscript.

Hour, Date, Place	Summary of Events and Information	Remarks and references to Appendices
11.8.15.	Visited Subsiding line & new Post at LA VESEE. Yeomanry Party working on wiring in afternoon. Cyclists by night. Lieut Godsall, 17 Co, ordered to take up duties of S.O.R.E to 3rd Corps. 8 Infantry Officers attached for instruction, 4 to 1st Wessex, 4 to 2nd Wessex Field Coys.	Gor
12.8.15.	Visited BOIS-GRENIER Post. & Subsidiary line. Visited Batteries with G.O.C. R.A. with reference to a proposed gun emplacement in 2nd Line. Det. 2nd Bridging Team ordered to move 7.0 a.m. on 13th.	Gor
13.8.15.	Det 2nd Bridging Team left at 7. a.m. to join 2nd Army. Inspected Subsidiary Line and Bois Grenier work on emplacement for Field Gun. Existing stock of Bricks needed. No more available for 3 weeks. 4 lorries of 27— D.A.P. stuck in NIEPPE FOREST whilst carting wire entanglement pickets. 84th Field Co. finished count of instruction with 17th Field Co.	Gor

Army Form C. 2118.

WAR DIARY
or
INTELLIGENCE SUMMARY

(Erase heading not required.)

Instructions regarding War Diaries and Intelligence Summaries are contained in F. S. Regs., Part II. and the Staff Manual respectively. Title pages will be prepared in manuscript.

Hour, Date, Place	Summary of Events and Information	Remarks and references to Appendices
14.8.15.	Visited Subsidiary line. Work on gaps in line for Counter-attack started on. Discussion with O.C. Divisional Train re. allotment of wagons. Supply of 9×3 timber getting short; units to exhibit to substitute 7×2½; large amount of which was purchased.	noon
15.8.15. 9.15am	Conference in G.O.C's Office. Work of salvage Section touched on and the obtaining of material from burnt houses.	
11.0 am	Special orders to contain no ashes to be taken of party is shelled.	
12 noon	G.O.C. ordered that all loose entanglement wire to be lowered below normal trajectory of bullets from parapet behind, where possible. Non-arrival of Det. 1st Bridging Train. Concern that we have not enough materials to complete more than 1 of our 3 Bridges.	fn

Army Form C. 2118.

WAR DIARY
or
INTELLIGENCE SUMMARY
(Erase heading not required.)

Instructions regarding War Diaries and Intelligence Summaries are contained in F. S. Regs., Part II. and the Staff Manual respectively. Title pages will be prepared in manuscript.

Hour, Date, Place	Summary of Events and Information	Remarks and references to Appendices
16.8.15.	Visited new communication trench to RUE DU BOIS and Subsidiary Line. Commenced work on Field Gun Emplacement in Subsidiary Line with R.A. Party. Departure of 2nd Bridging left us short of 6 Pontoons on our 3 Bridges. Bridging Train promised. Detachment from 1st Bridging Train promised. Bridge only complete. Major Norton Griffiths visited and informed us that Vertical Borers for testing substrata had been ordered. Demanded from RE Park but none available. Lieut Col. P.J.S. Radcliffe reported for 3 days course of instruction.	JSN
17.8.15.	Visited Front Line in Right Section with Lieut. Col. Radcliffe and took him round Shifts and Park. Visited Subsidiary Line & Ferme du Bois Communication Trench.	JSN
18.8.15.	Visited Front Line in Left Section with Lieut. Col. Radcliffe, and went over system of demanding Stores & purchasing & formation of Civilian Labour Gangs. Visited Subsidiary Line. Fire parapets to be made fightable between Breastworks. Work on Mine at RUE DU BOIS somewhat delayed by constant changing of Reliefs. Permanent Infantry Party of 32 asked for. Trucks from ISBERGUES Factory with steel girders have not arrived, and delay resulted in Machine Gun Emplacements. Enquiries made.	JSN

Army Form C. 2118.

WAR DIARY
or
INTELLIGENCE SUMMARY

(Erase heading not required.)

Instructions regarding War Diaries and Intelligence Summaries are contained in F. S. Regs., Part II. and the Staff Manual respectively. Title pages will be prepared in manuscript.

Hour, Date, Place	Summary of Events and Information	Remarks and references to Appendices
19.8.15.	Visited Subsidiary Line and PARK ROW Communication Trench. Enquiries as to trials of girders due to arrive show that they have not yet been delivered by Factory. Visited ISBERGUES. Detachment 1st Bridging Train arrived. Arrangements made to complete Pontoon Bridge. 1 Section only to 27th Division. Conference re pattern & size of steel girder for R.H. Gun Emplacements. Orders to treat immediately all Grenades by protecting junction of detonator & fuze with Latex.	RESR
20.8.15	Visited Subsidiary Line. Work on Machine Gun Emplacements to be pushed on. 1st Bridging Train started work on roads leading to Pontoon Bridges. 2/Lieut Barton joined 14th Field Co.	RESR
21.8.15.	Visited SHAFTESBURY AVENUE and Subsidiary Line. Shortage of wooden track for trench tramways. Discussion as to hastening supply of Muzzle Pivot Machine Gun mountings. Gravel supplied from GHQ reported unsatisfactory. Further trial with English cement ordered.	RESR

WAR DIARY or INTELLIGENCE SUMMARY

Army Form C. 2118.

(Erase heading not required.)

Instructions regarding War Diaries and Intelligence Summaries are contained in F.S. Regs., Part II. and the Staff Manual respectively. Title pages will be prepared in manuscript.

Hour, Date, Place	Summary of Events and Information	Remarks and references to Appendices
22.8.15.	Discussion as to steel plates required for Observing Stations. Pattern decided on and 100 plates purchased at LILLERS. 173rd Mining Co. require about 10 tons in iron weights to sink Caisson at RUE DU BOIS. Park could not supply; called for quotations. Two Officers fr. 181 Mining Co. reported. Arranged for billets for them. Co. Section from 20th Division joined 1st Wessex Field Co. for instruction.	JSW.
23.8.15.	Visited BOIS GRENIER Post & Subsidiary Line. Drainage and foot bands to be hastened. Mine netting still unobtainable. Asked C.E. to try and purchase. Yeomanry not available for work on Entanglement, owing to going into Trenches. Hostile Mining suspected in Trench 49. Arranged to sink a shaft and carry out listening.	JSW.
24.8.15.	Visited LA VESÉE & RUE FLEURIE Posts & Subsidiary Line. Work to pushed on in Posts and Infantry Party daily arranged for. C.E. decided not to purchase iron weights for RUE DU BOIS Mine, as they had been called out. No horses yet in R.E. Park; No 2 Army Workshop asked to supply. First Consignment of steel posts received. Lieut. H.M. Hance reported for duty with 181 Mining Co.	JSW.

Army Form C. 2118.

WAR DIARY
or
INTELLIGENCE SUMMARY
(Erase heading not required.)

Instructions regarding War Diaries and Intelligence Summaries are contained in F. S. Regs., Part II. and the Staff Manual respectively. Title pages will be prepared in manuscript.

Hour, Date, Place	Summary of Events and Information	Remarks and references to Appendices
25.8.15.	Inspection of Subsidiary Line and Headquarters "Dug-outs". Asten as to formation of "Labour Corps" issued. Green cards received. 2 Gendarmes reported for duty with Civilian Gangs. Shortage of gravel & slag for concrete. 181 Mining Co. started work with 173 Co. Asked CE for supply of small trees from NIEPPE FOREST. Lieut Piggott 1st Wessex Field Co. wounded.	Gsn.
26.8.15.	Inspection of new Assembly Trenches & Machine Gun Emplacements. "Orders for RE" issued and incorporated in 27th Division Defence Scheme. 17 Field Co. complained of shortage of transport for Trench Tramway. Obtained two lorries for their use daily. Inspection of Subsidiary Line and allotment of Gendarmes to Gangs.	Gsn.
27.8.15.	Inspection of new Assembly Trenches. Registration of civilian workmen for issue of Green Cards. Inspection of Subsidiary Line. New machine gun emplacements decided on.	Gsn.

WAR DIARY
or
INTELLIGENCE SUMMARY
(Erase heading not required.)

Army Form C. 2118.

Instructions regarding War Diaries and Intelligence Summaries are contained in F. S. Regs., Part II. and the Staff Manual respectively. Title pages will be prepared in manuscript.

Hour, Date, Place	Summary of Events and Information	Remarks and references to Appendices
28.8.15.	Visited BOIS-GRENIER & LA VESÉE Pats. Visited Timber Yard near BETHUNE to say if any of the wood being purchased for burning could be utilized in the Trenches. About 5 to 10 %/₀ might be useful. Shortage of Cement. Section of 20th Division left area, had been working with 1st Wessex.	ROR
29.8.15.	CE visited & discussed supply of materials. Reconnoitred new road for Field Ambulances near BOIS-GRENIER, and detailed a Civilian Gang for this work. Filling up green Cards for Airlines, & making out Nominal Rolls. CSM Ammon killed & one man wounded 17 Co RE.	ROR
30.8.15.	Visited Subsidiary line and new road near BOIS-GRENIER. Course for Infantry Officers with 17th Co. RE finished. 82.I.B relieved by 80 I.B. Pontoon Bridges placed in position & used by the Troops.	Sedn.

WAR DIARY
or
INTELLIGENCE SUMMARY

(Erase heading not required.)

Army Form C. 2118.

Hour, Date, Place	Summary of Events and Information	Remarks and references to Appendices
31.8.15.	Visited Subsidiary dump to new road at BOIS GRENIER. Masking gun emplacements with wire gauze and canvas. Serious shortage of any material for barbed wire entanglements & roads. Timber offered by PRUVOST FRERES at 225 francs per metre cube. CE asked if requisition may be resorted to. Shortage of wire nothing still apparent. Received offer of some from PARIS. CE agreed to buy. CE agreed to buy trucks & other materials by large document. Question of bringing up trucks & other materials by Trench Tramway in Detachment 111th Railway Co. started work on Right Section with 1st Wessex Field Co. 3rd Corps Workshops have been working for some days. They don't understand to supply anything to this Division.	

27th Division
R.E.

HdQrs R.E. 27th Division

Sept 15

CONFIDENTIAL.

WAR DIARY

of

HEADQUARTER 27TH DIVISIONAL ENGINEERS.

From. Sept. 1st 1915.

To Sept. 30th 1915.

Green
Lt. Col. R.E.
C.R.E. 27th Division

WAR DIARY
or
INTELLIGENCE SUMMARY

(Erase heading not required.)

Army Form C. 2118.

Instructions regarding War Diaries and Intelligence Summaries are contained in F. S. Regs., Part II. and the Staff Manual respectively. Title pages will be prepared in manuscript.

Hour, Date, Place	Summary of Events and Information	Remarks and references to Appendices
1.9.15.	Visited Subsidiary Line. Work on new road near BOIS-GRENIER nearly finished. Arranged for delivery of 100 tons slag for standings & roads. Units ask for 2000 tons. Arranged with Brigades re transport of stone to Trenches. Manufacture of portable bridge for Field Guns.	ESR
2.9.15.	Visited Subsidiary Line and BOIS=GRENIER posts. Drainage and footboards to be pushed on. G.O.C. RA inspected portable bridge and educed span to make of lights. Iron rails for Road Tramway not arrived and now urgently required. CE asked if we may purchase quarter as a transport of materials ensured, now that 3rd Corps dumps all materials for us at SAILLY, not in our area.	ESR
3.9.15	CRE went on leave calling 3rd Corps & GHQ on the way re Tramway. No work done on Subsidiary Line owing to weather. Conference as to pattern of Muzzle-Proof Machine Gun Mounting. Timber running very short. Visited ESTAIRES & MERVILLE to obtain. Conference with M.G. Officers of Brigades, & OC/MGS. Pattern of mounting decided on.	ESR

Army Form C. 2118.

WAR DIARY
or
INTELLIGENCE SUMMARY
(Erase heading not required.)

Instructions regarding War Diaries and Intelligence Summaries are contained in F. S. Regs., Part II. and the Staff Manual respectively. Title pages will be prepared in manuscript.

Hour, Date, Place	Summary of Events and Information	Remarks and references to Appendices
4.9.15.	Weather bad after 9.0. a.m. Very little work done by Civilian gangs. Experiments with darkened sandbags to screen loopholes, and with smoke balls ordered. Prismatic of tram path N. of R.LYS. for motor ambulances. Reinforcement of 6 men joined 17th Co. R.E.	gm
5.9.15.	Question of improving canvas shelters for winter use discussed. Arranged for supply of waste wood — "deckles" — for foot-boards. Large stock of timber of all sizes & corrugated iron at dockat MERVILLE. Stopped work on tow-path N. of R.LYS owing to wet weather; Arranged to supply party to make fascines for horse standings for Divisional Train.	mm
6.9.15.	Visited BOIS-GRENIER Post and Subsidiary line à LAVESSE. CE asked to make fascines for horse standings. Discussion of type of M.G. Emplacement in Defended localities. Visited HILLERS & ordered M.G. Mountings and ISBERGUES to order rails for trench tramway. Purchased last available nails. New positions required for 7 new Batteries of 23rd Division. G.S. told us to purchase.	bom

Army Form C. 2118.

WAR DIARY
or
INTELLIGENCE SUMMARY
(Erase heading not required.)

Instructions regarding War Diaries and Intelligence Summaries are contained in F. S. Regs., Part II. and the Staff Manual respectively. Title pages will be prepared in manuscript.

Hour, Date, Place	Summary of Events and Information	Remarks and references to Appendices
7.9.15.	Visited Subsidiary Line. Laid out new work on line W. of BOIS-GRENIER. Discussion as to conversion of existing Canvas Shelters into huts for winter use. Discussion & preparation of list of roads requiring repair in order of importance.	JSN
8.9.15. 10.30 a.m.	Preliminary Conference at 8th Division Head Quarters. G.O.C. 3rd Corps briefly outlined the operations of the next few weeks, and discussed precautions to be taken. 2nd Course for Infantry Officers with Field Companies commenced, 4 Officers with each Field Company. 102nd Field Company arrived for course of instruction with 17th Company. Arranged Billets. One man 181 Tunnelling Co., attached from 2nd Rifle Brigade, wounded.	JSN

WAR DIARY
or
INTELLIGENCE SUMMARY

(Erase heading not required.)

Army Form C. 2118.

Instructions regarding War Diaries and Intelligence Summaries are contained in F. S. Regs., Part II. and the Staff Manual respectively. Title pages will be prepared in manuscript.

Hour, Date, Place	Summary of Events and Information	Remarks and references to Appendices
9.9.15.	Visited Subsidiary Line. Screening M.G. Loopholes with wire gauze painted. Arranged for #2 Sections 102nd Co. R.E. to work with 1st Wessex Field Co., owing to difficulty of employing with 17th Co. R.E. CRE 23rd Division with 2nd Wessex Field Co. R.E. Mining inspected in Trench 61. Mining Officer sent down and reported nothing suspicious.	Ecn
10.9.15.	CRE 23rd Division visited and discussed allotment of Field Co. Knocked off all Civilian Gangs after 9.0. a.m. Visited MERVILLE and purchased timber for pikes and flooring of Shelters. Adjutant 23rd Division arrived and took over Billet. Discussed organisation of RE Park and Civilian Gangs.	non
11.9.15.	CRE 23rd Division visited and discussed work of Field Companies. Received orders for 128 Co. RE to be attached from 12th, & 102 Co R.E. to complete attachment on that date. Explained scheme for Ponton Bridges to Adjutant 23rd Division RE, & visited site of bridge & new road. Received orders to hand over to 23rd Division (27th Div. Operation Order No 57). Asked for 23rd Division Pontoons to be sent up early. O.C. 181 Co RE visited and asked for Party to sink shaft at I.15.2.2.5.	Ncn

Army Form C. 2118.

WAR DIARY
or
INTELLIGENCE SUMMARY.
(Erase heading not required.)

Instructions regarding War Diaries and Intelligence Summaries are contained in F.S. Regs., Part II and the Staff Manual respectively. Title pages will be prepared in manuscript.

Hour, Date, Place	Summary of Events and Information	Remarks and references to Appendices
12.9.15.	CRE 23rd Division visited. Explained system of Bridge and Labour Corps. 128 Co. RE arrived. 2 Sections attached to 17th Co and 2 to 1st Wessex. 10.2 Co. RE returned to 23rd Division Area. Ordered Field Co. to complete all equipment & be ready to move. All leave stopped until move to new area completed.	lsn
13.9.15.	HdQrs R.E. 23rd Division arrived at CROIX DU BAC. Commenced handing over Plans and Papers. Visited RE Park with Adjutant 23rd Divn RE. 27 Division Operation Order No 58 received, detailing moves to new Area. Companies notified. All men attached to 181 Mining Company R.E. to be transferred with exception of those belonging to Territorial Units.	lsn
14.9.15.	Handing over to CRE 23rd Division. Paying up Bills. Reinforcements of 12 men for 1st Wessex, & 12 for 2nd Wessex, arrived. R.E. Park taken over by 23rd Division.	
15.9.15.	Visited Subsidiary Line with Major Connor, 23rd Division, & explained system of working Civilians to him.	lsn

Army Form C. 2118.

WAR DIARY
or
INTELLIGENCE SUMMARY.

(Erase heading not required.)

Instructions regarding War Diaries and Intelligence Summaries are contained in F. S. Regs., Part II. and the Staff Manual respectively. Title pages will be prepared in manuscript.

Hour, Date, Place	Summary of Events and Information	Remarks and references to Appendices
16.9.15.	H'dQrs RE marched to MERRIS at 10.30.a.m., arriving at about 1.0.p.m. Adjutant left for new area with Party in Advance.	
17.9.15.	C.R.E. proceeded to new area at 12.0. noon with G.O.C.	
18.9.15.	H'dQrs RE moved at 4.30.a.m., joining 17th Field Co. at STRAZEELE, & entrained at THIENNES at 2.28.p.m. H'dQrs RE. CRE & Adjt visited new area with G.O.C and enquired about Mining. Reached GUILLAUCOURT at 2.30.a.m. Marched to LA MOTTE. CRE and Adjt. making enquiries re timber and RE. Stores with CE 12th Corps, and rejoined H'dQrs.	
19.9.15.		
20.9.15.	Discussion re formation of Brigade Mining Sections. Visit to Commandant French Engineers to settle Mining Questions. Received Operation Order No.60, detailing division of Line into 1/2 Sections.	
21.9.15.	H'dQrs RE marched at 10.15.a.m. and arrived at MERRICOURT at 12.15.p.m. Adjutant visited Mine Galleries & went into organization.	

(73989) W4141—463. 400,000. 9/14. H.&J.Ltd. Forms/C. 2118/10.

Army Form C. 2118.

WAR DIARY
or
INTELLIGENCE SUMMARY.
(Erase heading not required.)

Instructions regarding War Diaries and Intelligence Summaries are contained in F. S. Regs., Part II and the Staff Manual respectively. Title pages will be prepared in manuscript.

Hour, Date, Place	Summary of Events and Information	Remarks and references to Appendices
22.9.15.	Conference at Division H.Qrs at 8.0.a.m. Adjutant put in charge of Brigade Mining Sections, and to act as liaison Officer to the French. Visited French Stores and Company Offices. Arranged for Galleries Saliant, DOMPIERRE, to be evacuated, owing to suspected enemy mining underneath. French Stores at CHUIGNOLLES taken over by 2nd Wessex.	lsn
23.9.15.	Demanded Mining Stores. Arranged with Commandant, French Engineers, to leave 20 men with 1 Officer at FONTAINES LES CAPPY. Operation Order No 61 received. Line held by 27th Division extended to the right to the track FAY — FONTAINES LES CAPPY, including the whole of the FONTAINES LES CAPPY Mining Sector, and also the BOIS PHILIPPI area. 22nd Division Miners to remain for present. Arranged for supplies & rations of French Miners to be increased to represent fully their own scale. Arranged for 82nd Brigade Mining Section to join miners of 22nd Division. Arranged for 82nd Bgde. Mining Section to be employed in whole of & only in 27th Division area.	lsn
24.9.15.	Arranged for 80th & 81st Bgde Mining Sections to form at ECLUSIER and CAPPY respectively on 25th.	hon

Army Form C. 2118.

WAR DIARY
or
INTELLIGENCE SUMMARY.
(Erase heading not required.)

Instructions regarding War Diaries and Intelligence Summaries are contained in F.S. Regs., Part II and the Staff Manual respectively. Title pages will be prepared in manuscript.

Hour, Date, Place	Summary of Events and Information	Remarks and references to Appendices
25.9.15.	Visited 80th and 81st Bgde Mining Sections and arranged for them to work with French Gangs. Detailed men for Stores and Office, and arranged for instruction in listening. Visited 100th Co R.E. and 127th Co. R.E. & arranged for similar instruction of 82nd Bgde. Mining Section. Discussed general situation at FONTAINES LES CAPPY with French Officer.	JSR
26.9.15.	Arranged for shafts and to be sunk for 3 new galleries at GALLERIES Saillant, DOMPIERRE Sector, in case of a further test enemy offensive. Arranged for listener to go to suspected point outside FRISE mining area. Arranged for equipment for Mining Sections to be demanded.	JSR
27.9.15.	Decided to put 80th Bgde. Mining Section in dug-outs as soon as possible, owing to exposed position of their billets. Shortage of timber evident. Difficult to supply enough mining timber. 1st Wessex Field Co. at work on bridge over canal near CAPPY Lock. Lieut Cary rejoined 2nd Wessex from Hospital.	JSR

WAR DIARY
or
INTELLIGENCE SUMMARY.
(Erase heading not required.)

Army Form C. 2118.

Instructions regarding War Diaries and Intelligence Summaries are contained in F.S. Regs., Part II and the Staff Manual respectively. Title pages will be prepared in manuscript.

Hour, Date, Place	Summary of Events and Information	Remarks and references to Appendices
28.9.15.	Asked Brigades if further men likely to be available, or whether working parties would be detailed. Only parties available must come from Reserve Brigade, allotted for in rear, unless other urgent work in trenches is to cease. All French Companies reported excellent work done by Ogde Mining Sections.	WSR
29.9.15.	RE Park moved from MERICOURT to FROISSY. 108. Co. RE 22nd Division attached to 27th Division. 27th Division ordered to take over mining from 22nd Div. 2nd Wessex ordered to take over first from 127 Co. RE. Arranged with French to leave their Detachment till 2nd from 1st Wessex ordered to take over from 2nd Wessex.	WSR
30.9.15.	Arranged for meeting of O.C. 2nd Wessex & French Officer to discuss mining in sector taken over from 22nd Division. Arranged for 108 Co. to work on Defended localities in rear, and on roads. Bridge at CAPPY lock to be altered to allow passage of barges.	WSR

p.a. YPRES 1915 feb

CRE 27° Division. letter.

11.3.23.

My dear Edmonds

Yes Buckle is the name of the man. I remember it now. He & I were later, on (13° Sept-), the first "white" men to get on to Missy bridge over the Aisne — we saw no Germans, but the West Kent M.G. officer thought we were Germans & opened fire. He shot Buckles orderly in the leg & frightened us both to death!

Buckle was a very good chap —

West was an *official* despatch rider in command of some of those Varsity undergraduate D.R.s we had such on. He belonged to no less a man than the "Royal Arms & Supporters" on his hat; he was a good man & curiously enough I had him under me later, making roads in 2nd Corps Area behind Kemmel. He spoke French like a native & ran gangs of labourers — but knew little or nothing about roads, other than what his Common Sense told him. We made a good combination & the roads flourished!

the never lost his head or his temper
& was always smiling. I admired
his courage immensely. His staff
were as jumpy as all the rest.
He was the only man there who
knew what was going on, as all
the rest slept peacefully (!)
behind the Canal. I have talked
this show over with C. Romer who
was G.S.O.1 to the Canadians & I
discovered that even he did not
know the real situation. I suppose
his General did not either. I have
forgotten the details & dates, all
that is left to me is a very
close recollection of the horror
& , to me, useless slaughter.
The withdrawal to the chord
line through

2

I met old T Snow at the Club
the other day. I was in his (27th)
Divn as c/s later on. He tells me
Gen was during the 2nd Ypres battle
now. That was an unholy
show - the worst I was ever in.
So dangerous & so mismanaged.
Fools & S.O.s running about like
rabbits - thoroughly frightened
& fighting with each other I
presume. No method, no order,
Just murder of 1000 men for
want of a steady mind in
Command. Snow was the
only man who kept his head.
He lived in a dug out in
    Potze (I was with him)

3

Hooge was, I always thought, a horrible mistake. There were two alternatives viz. 1. to stay on the front-line. 2. To go back to the Canal line. The mid way line, chosen by GHQ from a map, which gave us certain ruling points to work on, was fatal. It was bad in every way. I know this as J & Seagin & Sankey laid it out between Hill 60 (5'0") & Frazenberg. We did it by daylight (lively job) & saw all its faults. I am sure we could have held the forward line quite easily, especially after my experience in the 1st Battle in Novr.

You see the pundits who

manoeuvered us. We've seen nor
knew how T.A. could fight
when he got a decent chance.
He never had a decent chance
at the time of which I write.
I often wonder who will put it
in the neck for wasting all those
lives, when the great Assize
comes along! I write all this
as, if you want information
from the only man who knows,
go to Snow. Paddy Reid shd know
but he was very jumpy —

Yours sincerely

B Waller

121/7381

Hdqrs RE. 27th Division

Part VII

Oct 15

CONFIDENTIAL

WAR DIARY

OF

HEADQUARTERS 27TH DIVISIONAL ENGINEERS

FROM: 1st Octr 1915

TO: 31st Octr 1915.

Nulle
Capt. RE
Adjutant 27th Divl Engrs
for CRE 27th Division

1/11/15.

WAR DIARY
or
INTELLIGENCE SUMMARY.
(Erase heading not required.)

Army Form C. 2118.

Instructions regarding War Diaries and Intelligence Summaries are contained in F.S. Regs., Part II. and the Staff Manual respectively. Title pages will be prepared in manuscript.

Hour, Date, Place	Summary of Events and Information	Remarks and references to Appendices
1.10.15.	Visited Brigades and asked for more guesses. 81st Bgde likely to have considerable number, 80th Bgde small number, 82nd Bgde very few. Arranged for Reserve Brigade to cut brushwood at MORCOURT and PROYART for hurdles. Arranged for stone for roads; supply from 12th Corps not due for some time. 2 men reported wounded 2nd Wessex R.E.	J.S.M
2.10.15.	Asked 80th Brigade for 6 reliefs of 24 men, each of 4 hours daily, to hasten on work in FRISE Sector. Unable to furnish, owing to reliefs. Arranged with Q Branch no equipment of Mining Sections and as to demanding reinforcements from Base to replace. Enemy blew mine at FONTAINES LES CAPPY, 3 men 2nd Wessex R.E. lost.	J.S.M
3.10.15.	Arranged with 82nd Brigade to supply party of 60 to form trenches for evacuation of earth on new galleries at DOMPIERRE. 80th Brigade unable to supply working party owing to other urgent work. Arranged with French to leave four skilled men, well acquainted with FONTAINES LES CAPPY Sector, with 2nd Wessex for a week, and for late French O.C. to visit daily.	J.S.M

WAR DIARY
or
INTELLIGENCE SUMMARY.
(Erase heading not required.)

Army Form C. 2118.

Hour, Date, Place	Summary of Events and Information	Remarks and references to Appendices
4.10.15.	Arranged for guard over dynamite stores near CAPPY. Arranged with 81st Brigade to supply working parties to assist miners at DOMPIERRE. 81st Brigade relieved 82nd Brigade in front line. 1 man wounded 1st Wessex RE and 1 man 17th Co. RE.	
5.10.15.	Adjt Visited DOMPIERRE Mining sector and arranged for work to be done by working parties. CRE visited FRISE Sector of Line with O.C. 17 Co. RE. 2nd Wessex RE relieved 100th Co. RE in PHILIPPI Mine Sector.	WF
6.10.15.	Enemy mines fired at 10 p.m. and 9.5 p.m. Latter formed a crater. Enemy miners very active. Arranged with S.S.O. for supply of candles, oil & for mines as C.E. cannot supply us for a fortnight. Also arranged supply of coal for saws.	WF
7.10.15.	Asked 90 I.B. to send all miners (52) in their additional lot, asked 81 I.B. to send ditto (236). Arranged with 81 I.B. to have 30 men at Galenu Saliens, Dompierre sector and 10 men at Peuplier Saliens, to keep in the "boyaux d'evacuation" from the new Shafts in these Saliens.	WF

WAR DIARY
or
INTELLIGENCE SUMMARY.
(Erase heading not required.)

Army Form C. 2118.

Instructions regarding War Diaries and Intelligence Summaries are contained in F. S. Regs., Part II. and the Staff Manual respectively. Title pages will be prepared in manuscript.

Hour, Date, Place	Summary of Events and Information	Remarks and references to Appendices
8.10.15	The parties arranged for yesterday commenced work	WK
9.10.15	Wrote C.E. asking to arrange for "photo apparatus" having been ordered list of plant for mining. School to C.E.	WK
10.10.15	152 men only (those who have had some mining experience) to report from 1 I.B. by instructions G.S. Lewis informed Standard in his position. Informed 21 I.B. as to position of explosive stores in this area.	WK
11.10.15	Arranged for lots to go to place of the mining parties subs. laying at MARCELCAVE. Arranged with 2nd Army Wessex Field Coy to send 3 men to photo school and arranged for with chemical adviser 3rd Army.	WK
12.10.15	Arranged transport for our daily supply of 13000 sandbags from No.6 R.E. Park ACHEUX. Also transport for photo sets from BEAUQUESNE. 18th Sanitary Company reported to Corps.	WK
13.10.15	Day went went on locm. Arranged for machine gun mountings to be sent by rail from WILLERS as no motor transport available for the purpose	WK

Army Form C. 2118.

WAR DIARY
or
INTELLIGENCE SUMMARY.
(Erase heading not required.)

Instructions regarding War Diaries and Intelligence Summaries are contained in F.S. Regs., Part II. and the Staff Manual respectively. Title pages will be prepared in manuscript.

Hour, Date, Place	Summary of Events and Information	Remarks and references to Appendices
14.10.15	Arranged transport for our store of shirts at MARCELCAVE.	WR
15.10.15	Arranged with Col. Cornus (Genie Francaise) for the purchase of 5000 steel pickets from AMIENS.	WR
16.10.15	Arranged with ADRT Northern area to have machine gun mountings brought from LILLERS.	WR
17.10.15	Convoy left exploded by French miners in this area at 8.30am carrying a small crater to be formed. Gauge will be available on 19th to bring pickets from AMIENS to FROISSY.	WR
18.10.15	Informed batteries that no crosses are available in this district for the purpose of constructing horse standings.	WR
19.10.15	Went to Amiens and paid outstanding bills. Arranged with 1N.T. for transport of more timber from Amiens to Froissy. Purchased a planing machine at Amiens, and placed order for 5000 pickets arranged on in 15th.	WR
20.10.15	Leave again stopped in the division. No transport will be available tomorrow.	WR

WAR DIARY
or
INTELLIGENCE SUMMARY.
(Erase heading not required.)

Army Form C. 2118.

Hour, Date, Place			Summary of Events and Information	Remarks and references to Appendices
21.	10.	15.	Started to collect stores & to return them to No. 6 R.E. Park, MERICOURT L'ABBE & to MARCELCAVE, in anticipation of coming move. Informed AMIENS firms regarding cancelling of orders placed. 2nd I.B. Mining Schm ordered to rejoin their units. Wired companies to collect stores & return to FROISSY and also to return horse rollers to No.6 Park.	W.B.
22.	10.	16.	Continued collection and return of stores. Wrote C.E. 10 Corps asking if he will take over timber ordered from AMIENS. The C.R.E. 5th (R) Division will take over all timber and stores at FROISSY. Cleared office CORBIE bills & settled with Maire de la Commune de MORCOURT for timber cut during last 3 months. Leave again started in the division.	W.B.
23.	10.	15.	Stopped daily supply of petrol, candles &c from S.S.O. Cleared off all AMIENS bills	W.B.
24.	10.	15.	1st/West Kent left MERICOURT 2nd/Wessex left CHUIGNOLLES	
25.	10.	15.	Headquarters R.E. moved at 7.30 a.m. to BOVES arriving about 1.0. p.m. CRE remained at MERICOURT to hand over.	W.B.

Army Form C. 2118.

WAR DIARY
or
INTELLIGENCE SUMMARY.
(Erase heading not required.)

Instructions regarding War Diaries and Intelligence Summaries are contained in F.S. Regs., Part II and the Staff Manual respectively. Title pages will be prepared in manuscript.

Hour, Date, Place	Summary of Events and Information	Remarks and references to Appendices
26.10.15.	Headquarters R.E. marched at 7.30. a.m. to BOUVELLES. CRE arrived direct from MERICOURT.	lsn
27.10.15.	Reallotment of Billets in BOUVELLES.	lsn
28.10.15.	Adjutant returned from sick leave.	lsn
29.10.15.	Visit 2nd Wessex Field Co. and 17th Co. Billeting satisfactory.	lsn
30.10.15.	CRE went on leave.	lsn
31.10.15.	All men on leave must be back by evening of 9th Nov^2. CRE ordered to be back by 5th Nov^2.	lsn

19/7429

VII
2/9/19

H.Q. R.E., 27th Div.

CONFIDENTIAL

WAR DIARY
OF
HEADQUARTERS 27TH DIVISIONAL ENGINEERS

FROM Nov 1st 1915.

TO Nov 30th 1915.

[signature]
Lieut. Col. R.E.
C.R.E. 27th Division

Army Form C. 2118.

WAR DIARY
or
INTELLIGENCE SUMMARY

(Erase heading not required.)

Instructions regarding War Diaries and Intelligence Summaries are contained in F. S. Regs., Part II. and the Staff Manual respectively. Title pages will be prepared in manuscript.

Hour, Date, Place	Summary of Events and Information	Remarks and references to Appendices
1.11.15.	Division at rest. Awaiting orders. Hd. Qrs. at BOVELLES.	
5.11.15.	All heavy-draught horses of Field Cos. exchanged for L.D. Mules. Hd. Qrs. drew 1 pair lead mules for Cook's Cart.	
7.11.15.	Farrier Sgt. Stevens, 17th Co. R.E., presented with Medaille Militaire. Reinforcement of 24 men arrived for 1st Wessex R.E.	
8.11.15.	2/Lieut T.A. Ross joined 17th Co. R.E.	
10.11.15.	2/Lieut R.A. Williams left 17th Co R.E. to join 20th A.T.C. R.E.	
11.11.15.	Exchange of L.D. Horses for Mules by Field Cos.	
16.11.15.	Lieut. C.A. Coombes rejoined 17th Co. R.E. from Base.	
17.11.15.	2/Lieut. T.A. Ross left 17th Co. R.E. to join 1st Field Co. R.E.	
21.11.15.	Reinforcement of 21 drivers for 17th Co R.E. and 3 drivers for Hd. Qrs. R.E. arrived.	

Army Form C. 2118.

WAR DIARY
or
INTELLIGENCE SUMMARY
(Erase heading not required.)

Instructions regarding War Diaries and Intelligence Summaries are contained in F. S. Regs., Part II. and the Staff Manual respectively. Title pages will be prepared in manuscript.

Hour, Date, Place	Summary of Events and Information	Remarks and references to Appendices
24.11.15.	1 Officer 1st Wessex and 1 Officer 2nd Wessex detailed for entraining duties at LONGUEAU Station.	eon
26.11.15.	Reinforcement of ~~Staff~~ 3 mounted NCOs and 1 Shoeing smith joined 17th Field Co. RE from Base.	eon
30.11.15.	Division still at rest. HdQrs at BOVELLES.	eon

CONFIDENTIAL.

WAR DIARY

OF

HEADQUARTERS 27TH DIVISIONAL ENGINEERS

Vol VIII

From Dec 1st 1915
To Dec. 31st 1915

[signature]
Capt. RE
for CRE 27th Division

WAR DIARY
or
INTELLIGENCE SUMMARY

(Erase heading not required.)

Army Form C. 2118.

Hour, Date, Place	Summary of Events and Information	Remarks and references to Appendices
1.12.15.	Division at rest. Hd.Qrs. at BOYELLES.	GSN.
5.12.15.	Orders received for all RE to entrain at LONGUEAU Station on 7th inst.	GSN
6.12.15.	1st and 2nd Wessex Field Companies moved to new Billets at CLERY. 1/4th Co. remain at FLUY.	GSN
7.12.15.	Hd.Qrs. RE. marched at 12.0. noon to entrain at LONGUEAU Station. Hd.Qrs RE, 1/4th Co. RE, 1/1st Wessex Field Co. RE started entraining at 4.25.p.m. Train left at 6.35.p.m. 2nd Wessex RE and 1/1st Wessex RE commenced entraining at 6.20.p.m.	GSN
9.12.15.	Arrival at PRADO Station, MARSEILLE, at 6.0.p.m. 2nd Wessex and 1/1st Wessex arrived at DOCKS Station about 5.30 p.m. All RE Units went into Camp at EXHIBITION Camp.	GSN

Army Form C. 2118.

WAR DIARY
or
INTELLIGENCE SUMMARY

(Erase heading not required.)

Instructions regarding War Diaries and Intelligence Summaries are contained in F. S. Regs., Part II. and the Staff Manual respectively. Title pages will be prepared in manuscript.

Hour, Date, Place	Summary of Events and Information	Remarks and references to Appendices
12.12.15.	All R.E. moved to BORELY Camp at 2.0. p.m. Awaiting orders.	Lieu
29.12.15.	Hd Qrs R.E. to embark with Divisional Hd Qrs about the 31st.	Lieu
30.12.15.	Dismounted portions of Field Conference to be held in readiness to embark with Divisional Hd Qrs about the 1st Jany. Pontoon and Trestle Wagons to be embarked without horses on the 31st, with party of 4 men.	Lieu

Army Form C. 2118.

WAR DIARY
or
INTELLIGENCE SUMMARY
(Erase heading not required.)

Hour, Date, Place	Summary of Events and Information	Remarks and references to Appendices
31.12.15.	"Embarkation Programme — 1.1.16." received. H'd Q'rs R.E. to embark at 2.0. p.m. on that day. One officer from each Field Co., with 2 batmen each, to be attached to H'd Q's.	

www.ingramcontent.com/pod-product-compliance
Lightning Source LLC
Chambersburg PA
CBHW081555160426
43191CB00011B/1937